Searchlight
BOOKS™

What's Amazing about Space?

Exploring the
International
Space Station

Laura Hamilton Waxman

Lerner Publications Company
Minneapolis

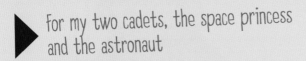

For my two cadets, the space princess
and the astronaut

Lerner Publications Company
A division of Lerner Publishing Group, Inc.
241 First Avenue North
Minneapolis, MN 55401 U.S.A.

Website address: www.lernerbooks.com

Library of Congress Cataloging-in-Publication Data

Waxman, Laura Hamilton.
  Exploring the international space station / by Laura Hamilton Waxman.
    p.   cm. — (Searchlight books™—What's amazing about space?)
  Includes index.
  ISBN 978-0-7613-5443-7 (lib. bdg. : alk. paper)
  1. Space stations—Juvenile literature. 2. Astronautics—International cooperation—Juvenile literature. I. Title.
  TL797.15.W39 2012
  629.44'2—dc22   2010035394

Manufactured in the United States of America
1 – DP – 7/15/11

Contents

Chapter 1

A HOME IN SPACE

Imagine waking up in a sleeping bag. But you aren't in a tent. You aren't even on the ground. You're attached to a wall. Outside your window lies the bright, blue Earth. You float out of your sleeping bag to start the day. It's just another morning on the International Space Station (ISS).

A view of Earth from space. What do people aboard the ISS see when they look out their windows?

Big and Fast

The ISS flies 240 miles (386 kilometers) above our planet. It circles Earth at 17,200 miles (27,720 km) per hour. Each full circle around Earth is called an orbit. An orbit takes ninety minutes.

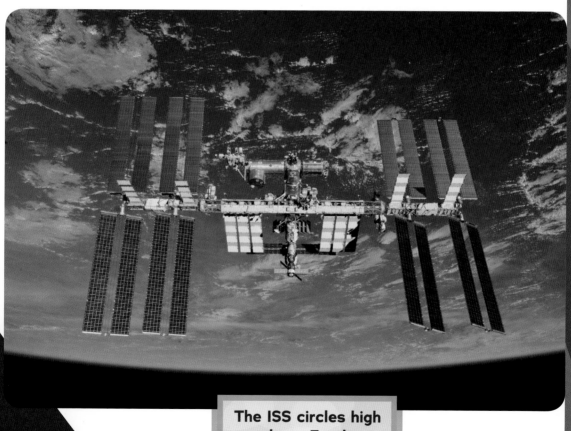

The ISS circles high above Earth.

Thousands of parts make up the ISS. The biggest parts are called modules. Many of the modules are like rooms. The station has modules for sleeping, working, and storing supplies. The modules have names such as *Destiny*, *Harmony*, and *Unity*.

A robot arm moves the *Destiny* module from a space shuttle to the ISS.

The crews of the ISS and the space shuttle *Discovery* pose on the ISS in April 2010.

Astronauts live and work on the space station. These people are trained to travel in outer space. ISS astronauts come from countries such as the United States, Russia, Brazil, Japan, and the Netherlands.

Countries Coming Together

In 1984, the United States asked other nations to help it build the world's biggest space station. Japan, Canada, Brazil, and eleven European nations agreed to take part. Later, Russia joined in. Russia and the United States had been rivals for many years. The ISS helped bring them together.

ISS and space shuttle astronauts work on the *Zarya* module in 1998. The first ISS crew included two Russians and one American.

Russia built the first part of the ISS. It went into orbit in 1998. Since then, more parts have been added each year. The parts are built on Earth. Astronauts put them together in space.

An astronaut connects parts of the ISS in 1998.

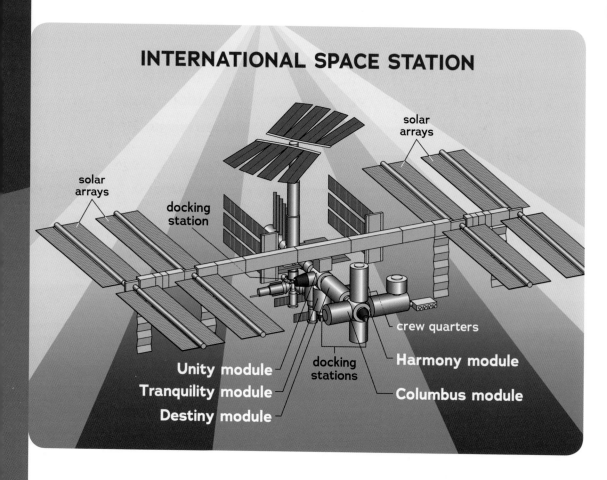

INTERNATIONAL SPACE STATION

solar arrays

solar arrays

docking station

crew quarters

Unity module

Tranquility module

Destiny module

docking stations

Harmony module

Columbus module

The space station is huge. When complete, it will measure 356 feet (109 meters) wide. It will weigh around 800,000 pounds (362,874 kilograms). That's as long as a football field and as heavy as 450 cars.

Chapter 2

JOBS FOR EVERYONE

Two members of the ISS crew work in the *Destiny* laboratory in 2010. Can you guess how long they stayed on the ISS?

Since 2000, hundreds of astronauts have worked on the ISS. They arrive in small teams. Each team is made up of astronauts from at least two countries. The men and women who run the station are its crew. The crew changes about every six months.

Low Gravity

ISS astronauts spend more than eighteen months training on Earth. They learn how to use and repair the station's equipment. Some of them learn how to build the ISS. They also practice living with very little gravity.

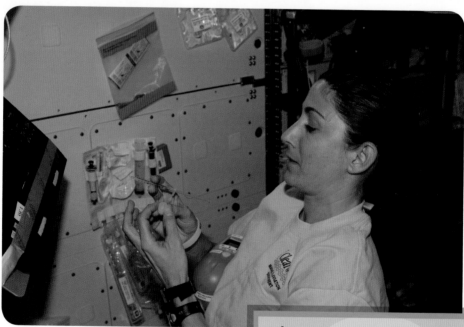

An astronaut tests water quality on the ISS. People living on the ISS must make sure every part of the station is working properly.

Gravity is the force that pulls one object toward another. Earth's gravity keeps objects on the ground. You can jump up. But gravity always pulls you back down.

Astronauts on the ISS live in weightlessness. The station has no up or down. Astronauts don't walk or run. They fly and float around the space station. Loose objects float too.

Fruit floats around with these astronauts aboard the ISS in 2008.

Space Scientists

The space station has a crew of six astronauts. These men and women take care of the ISS. They keep computers and other equipment working properly.

The crew of the ISS must know how to operate all the station's equipment.

A member of the ISS crew shows a plant experiment in one of the labs on the ISS. The plant they are growing is barley, a kind of grain.

The crew also works in the station's laboratories. They use tools and machines to do experiments there.

The experiments test scientific ideas. Crew members learn how things work in weightlessness. They study how plants grow in space. Crew members even study themselves. They learn how being in space changes the human body.

This experiment helps crew members study plant growth in space.

What the astronauts learn can help people on Earth. The astronauts study ways to make better medicines. They do experiments on materials such as metals and glass. These tests could help create stronger buildings on Earth. The astronauts learn more about our planet by studying it from space too.

A crew member works the controls for one of the station's robotic arms. Robotic arms help astronauts do experiments and other tasks in space.

Astronauts go on space walks outside the ISS. They fix the equipment on the station and keep it in good condition.

Space Walks

Some astronauts come to the ISS for days instead of months. Their job is to add parts to the space station. These builders must work outside the station. To do this, they have to go on space walks.

Outer space is a deadly place for humans. There's no air to breathe. Temperatures are freezing cold in the darkness and boiling hot in sunlight. The Sun's rays are very harmful to humans. Space suits and helmets protect the astronauts.

This astronaut is wearing a space suit and a helmet. Every part of an astronaut's body must be protected from the dangers of space.

Astronauts on space walks are weightless. So they stay strapped to the ISS at all times. But what if someone gets loose?

A SPECIAL TOOL KEEPS THIS ASTRONAUT ATTACHED TO THE ISS. ASTRONAUTS MUST BE CONNECTED TO THE STATION AT ALL TIMES.

Can you see the backpack-type equipment on this astronaut? It's called a SAFER.

All spacewalkers wear a small flying machine called a SAFER. SAFER stands for Simplified Aid for EVA Rescue. (EVA stands for extravehicular activity.) The SAFER straps to the back of the space suit like a backpack. It can shoot jets of air that push an astronaut back to safety.

Chapter 3

SUPPLYING THE ISS

The ISS and its crew need lots of supplies. But space doesn't have any grocery stores or hardware stores. Spacecraft must carry supplies from Earth to the ISS. They also carry astronauts. Spacecraft usually come to the station every one to three months.

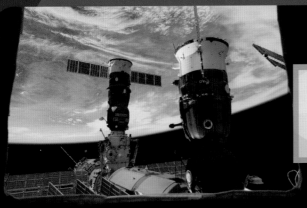

A Russian spacecraft docks with the ISS. How does the ISS crew get its supplies?

Food

Astronauts need food on the ISS. The space station doesn't have a refrigerator. So most of the food is canned or dried.

This meal is dried and covered in plastic wrap. A scissors comes with the meal so that astronauts can open the plastic wrap.

Astronauts eat everything from chicken to brownies. They also have drinks such as coffee, tea, and orange juice. Space drinks come as powders. Astronauts add water to drinks and dried food at mealtime.

Russian members of the ISS crew share a meal.

Water

Water also is shipped from Earth. But spacecraft can't carry nearly as much water as the astronauts need. So the space station has machines for making drinking water. These machines turn sweat, shower water, and urine into clean drinking water. It may sound gross. But it works!

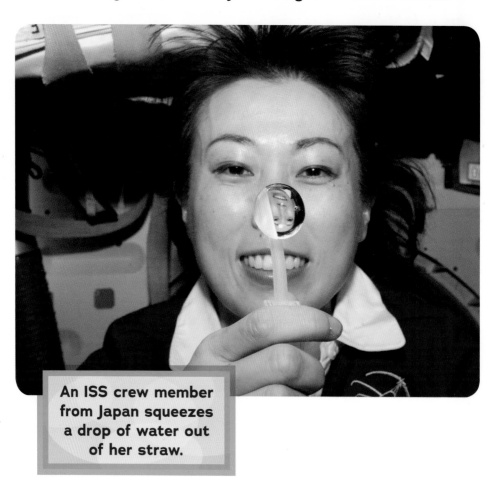

An ISS crew member from Japan squeezes a drop of water out of her straw.

PANELS ON THE WINGS OF THE ISS
CAPTURE SUNLIGHT. THEY USE IT TO
CREATE POWER FOR THE STATION.

Electricity

The ISS needs power for its equipment. The space
station makes its own power. It uses its solar arrays.
These sunlight collectors look like big wings. They turn
sunlight into electricity.

Chapter 4

A DAY IN THE LIFE

Life on the space station is busy. Each crew member has different jobs each day. But the crew usually follows the same schedule. They wake up each morning around six. They go to sleep by nine thirty in the evening. In between is a full day of activity.

This astronaut is holding directions for how to run equipment on the ISS. Crew members spend a lot of time using and caring for equipment. What else does the crew do each day?

INTERNATIONAL SPACE STATION

ROBOTICS FS

PLEASE RETURN ON STS-120

Mealtime

The crew often comes together for breakfast, lunch, and dinner. But they don't sit around the table. Instead, they slip their feet into footholds on the floor. These straps or bars keep them in one place.

A visiting crew from a spacecraft joins the ISS crew for a meal. The ISS can get crowded when extra people are aboard.

Crew members share a meal in the *Unity* module. Food containers are attached to a food tray so they don't float away.

Everything on the table must be tied down. Food trays are strapped to the table. Many of the food containers have sticky Velcro on the bottom. Magnets keep knives and forks from floating away.

The crew tries not to spill anything. Liquid and food in weightlessness can float into the space station's equipment.

Crew members are careful not to let food float away from them and into the equipment!

Staying Strong

Crew members work from ten to twelve hours on most days. They take exercise breaks in the morning and the afternoon. Exercising helps astronauts stay healthy. Their bodies don't have to fight against gravity. So moving around takes much less work. Over time, their muscles and bones grow weak.

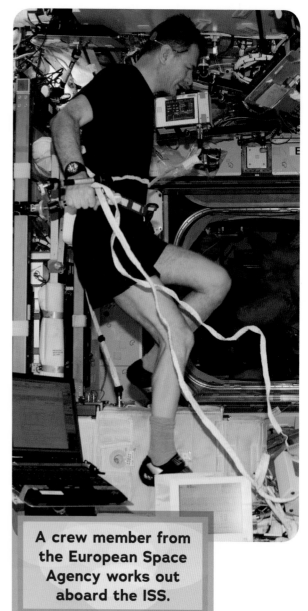

A crew member from the European Space Agency works out aboard the ISS.

Exercise helps with this problem. The ISS has treadmills for running. It has an exercise bike without a seat. And it has a machine for lifting weights.

This crew member works out on the station's exercise bike. Exercise is important to keep crew members healthy.

Time to Relax

The crew finishes work around seven thirty in the evening. They eat dinner. Then they have free time. They can watch a movie, e-mail family back home, strum a guitar, or just relax. There's even a phone to call family members on Earth.

This astronaut relaxes on the ISS by playing his guitar. He can also enjoy the view of Earth out the space station's windows.

Sleep

Each member of the crew has a sleeping area. But you won't find a bed there. Astronauts sleep in special sleeping bags. The bags are strapped to a wall.

ISS crew members zip themselves into their sleeping bags and say good night at the end of the day.

Chapter 5

THE FUTURE OF THE ISS

The space station won't last forever. It costs a lot of money to keep it running. Even so, the United States and other countries hope to use it until at least 2020. There's a lot more to learn about life in space.

The ISS is an important tool for learning about space. How long will it remain in space?

Dreaming New Dreams

Many new experiments are planned for the space station's laboratories. And the ISS is still teaching us about how to survive in space. These lessons may allow people to live even farther from Earth. Someday we could build stations on the Moon or Mars. The work on the ISS could make these dreams come true.

Earth is shown in the sky in this artist's drawing of a base on the Moon.

Glossary

astronaut: a person trained to travel in space

crew: the astronauts who live on and operate the International Space Station for months at a time

gravity: the force that pulls one object toward another

laboratory: an area set aside for scientific experiments

module: a part of the space station where people live, work, and store supplies

orbit: a full circle around Earth

SAFER: Simplified Aid for EVA (extravehicular activity) Rescue. The SAFER is a machine that straps to the back of a space suit. It can shoot jets of air that fly a person a short distance in space.

solar array: a part of the space station that turns sunlight into electricity

spacecraft: a vehicle that carries people and supplies to outer space

space walk: the job of moving and working outside in space

Learn More about the International Space Station

Books

Baker, David, and Heather Kissock. *International Space Station*. New York: Weigl Publishers, 2009. Read about the International Space Station, its uses, and possible future.

Bredeson, Carmen. *What Do Astronauts Do?* Berkeley Heights, NJ: Enslow Elementary, 2008. This book gives readers a window into the work of space travelers.

McCarthy, Meghan. *Astronaut Handbook*. New York: Alfred A. Knopf, 2008. Follow four future astronauts as they go through training.

Waxman, Laura Hamilton. *Exploring Space Travel*. Minneapolis: Lerner Publications Company, 2012. Explore the work and life of astronauts and tourists in space.

Websites

Clickable Spacesuit
http://www.nasa.gov/audience/foreducators/spacesuits/home/clickable_suit.html
Learn about everything a spacewalker needs to stay safe.

Space Station Kids
http://iss.jaxa.jp/kids/en/station/01.html
Visit this website for fun facts about the space station and life in space.

Station Spacewalk Game
http://www.nasa.gov/multimedia/3d_resources/station_spacewalk_game.html
Find out how hard it can be to build the ISS in space by playing this online game.

Index

Photo Acknowledgments

The images in this book are used with the permission of: NASA/JSC, pp. 4, 5, 6, 7, 8, 9, 11, 12, 13, 14, 15, 17, 18, 21, 22, 23, 25, 26, 28, 29, 30, 31, 32, 33, 34, 35, 36, © Laura Westlund/Independent Picture Service, p. 10; © NASA Handout/Getty Images, p. 27; © NASA/Photo Researchers, Inc., pp. 16, 20, 24; © Science Source/Photo Researchers, Inc., p. 19; © Chris Butler/Photo Researchers, Inc., p. 37. Front Cover: NASA/JSC.

Main body text set in Adrianna Regular 14/20
Typeface provided by Chank

To...*Baby Cashion*

Cannot wait to meet you! Hugs,
Bob & Debbie Cannucci

The Littlest Bunny invites
you on an
Easter Adventure

an Easter Adventure

The Littlest Bunny in North Carolina

MAY

JOE

Written by Lily Jacobs
Illustrated by Robert Dunn and Jerry Pyke
Designed by Sarah Allen

Published by Sourcebooks Jabberwocky, an imprint of Sourcebooks, Inc.
P.O. Box 4410, Naperville, Illinois 60567-4410
(630) 961-3900
Fax: (630) 961-2168
jabberwockykids.com

Date of Production: December 2016
Run Number: HTW_PO020916
Printed and bound in China (GD)
10 9 8 7 6 5 4 3

an Easter Adventure

The Littlest Bunny in North Carolina

Written by Lily Jacobs
Illustrated by Robert Dunn

sourcebooks
jabberwocky

Not long ago, in a land you might know,
Lived a girl named May and a boy named Joe.

WELCOME TO NORTH CAROLINA

They had moved to North Carolina, and longed to explore,
Make new friends, have adventures, and many things more!

North Carolina Pet Store

On the day before Easter,
they rode into town.
They went to the pet store
and looked all around.

There in the front
was a pen full of bunnies.
The small ones were cute,
and the big ones were funny.

They played with the bunnies
and thought for a bit,
And then they agreed
on the most *perfect* fit:

The *littlest* bunny,
with the sweetest small hop.

"He's ours!" May announced.
"Let's call him Flop."

So Flop joined the family
that sunny spring day.
The littlest bunny
was now home to stay.

They played with the bunny until it was late,
Then settled Flop into his cozy, snug crate.

May gave Flop a kiss
and Joe patted his head,
And then the two children
both climbed into bed.

A soft evening breeze blew in through the window,
And May and Joe smiled as they slept on their pillows.

But Flop had no time now
to close his own eyes:
He was preparing
an Easter surprise!

He was quite little,
that much was true,
But tonight our dear Flop
had a big job to do.

For he had a secret
he hadn't let show:

He was the Easter Bunny, and he had to go!

A magical wind gave his whiskers a tickle.
His nose, how it twitched! His ears, how they wiggled!

Soon, Flop was quite different than ever before.
And he couldn't wait—not for one moment more!

He raced through the house and out into the night,
To where he had hidden his eggs out of sight.

His marvelous burrow held Easter eggs plenty:
To be quite exact, nine million and twenty!
He packed up the eggs; he looked at the map.
He fastened his goggles and his red flying cap.

Then Flop hopped right into
his hot air balloon,
And soon he was soaring
as high as the moon!

As he watched his first stop grow nearer and nearer,
His Tar Heel State mission became even clearer.

First, Flop balanced eggs
on a tall building top...

...Then he went to
the park, spreading
eggs as he hopped.

And then he dashed off
for an Easter home run...

...Then quietly hid
chocolate eggs, one by one.

With big bounces here and
giant jumps there,

Flop hid **North Carolina's eggs** everywhere!

WEST   EAST

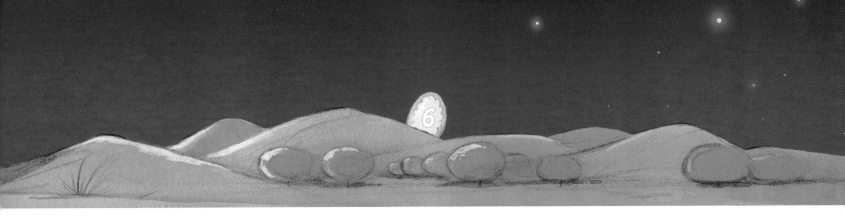

He flew to the **east**, to the **south**,
west, and **north**.
He crisscrossed the state; he raced
back and **forth**.

Asheville and Raleigh and Charlotte got treats,
Then Durham and Greensboro too were complete.

Fayetteville, Wilmington—the long list went on.
Flop was delivering his eggs until dawn!

Finally, Flop found his very last stop.
He came to *your* house with a bounce and a hop!
And there he delivered his Easter surprises:
So many eggs, of all shapes and sizes!
And when he was done,
he stopped for a rest.

16

Yes, surely this Easter
was one of his best!

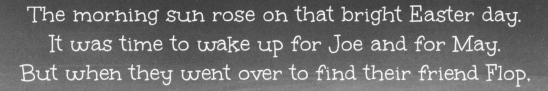

The morning sun rose on that bright Easter day.
It was time to wake up for Joe and for May.
But when they went over to find their friend Flop,

The door was wide open—
his crate was unlocked!

There were eggs to discover, as all children know.
"But we just want Flop!" cried May and cried Joe.

They looked under their beds; they looked all around.
But the littlest bunny just couldn't be found.

But whose goggles were these?

Who unfolded this map?

Then from 'round the corner came a faint *tap-tap-tap*.
They rushed and they stumbled. It had to be him!
And there they found baskets—
and something else was tucked in?

"It's Flop!" they cried out, and held him so close.
Joe tickled his ears and May kissed his pink nose.
Flop hugged them back, his new friends so dear.

Happy Easter, North Carolina!
See you next year!

Did you find all the Easter eggs
hidden in North Carolina?
Look back through the book to see
if you can spot all 20 eggs.

Give up?
Check the answers
on the last page.